Minnesota State Capitol

St. Paul

Jane Moorman

There is a saying, "It was a Friday night, and it seemed like a good idea at the time." That sums up the beginning of the State Capitols Project.

When photographer Jane Moorman told her brother of her idea of photographing state capitols, he said, "You do know there are 50 states and two of them you can't drive to."

Her answer was, "Your point is? It gives me a good reason to visit every state."

Minnesota: The North Star State

Minnesota's capitol, the third since statehood in 1858, was selected from 40 submitted designs in 1895. Local architect Cass Gilbert's Italian Renaissance style was selected. Construction began in 1896 and was completed in 1905.

Gilbert envisioned marble and bronze statuary on the exterior and numerous works of art in the interior. In a 1901 architect's report, Gilbert noted his vision for the art:

"Nothing will give the building greater distinction or lend more to its educational value and to the evidence of the advancement of civilization and intelligence of the State than the recognition of the arts as represented by the great painters and sculptors of the present day."

When the capitol opened in 1906, there were roughly 60 works of art. Over the years, artwork was added; by 2017, the total reached 150.

Much of the art planned for the capitol was allegorical, as expressed through murals. Some of the art was controversial in the 1900s, with multiple groups demanding that the artwork in the capitol illustrate historic events of Minnesota's past.

A restoration project from 2013 to 2017 brought the capitol's many works of art back to their original array of brilliant colors after being freed from their decades of grime accumulated from smoke, coal dust and other impurities.

Gold-Gilded Quadriga

Adorning the south entrance of the capitol are the statues Progress of the State, and the *Six Virtues* sculpted by Daniel Chester French and Edward Clark Potter.

Progress of the State is the Columbus Quadriga, a statue depicting Christopher Columbus standing in a four-horse chariot guided by two maidens carrying staffs of victory.

The horses represent the power of nature: earth, wind, fire and water.

Progress of the States

Six Virtue statues: Truth, Integrity, Prudence, Courage, Bounty and Wisdom.

Dome Crowned In Gold

The Italian Renaissance architectural style capitol designed by architect Cass Gilbert is covered with White Georgia marble and St. Cloud granite veneer.

The gold-leaf ball atop the White Georgia marble dome's lantern is 223 feet above the ground.

The windows in the dome help illuminate the inner dome and the rotunda at the center of the building.

Rotunda

A crystal chandelier with 92 lights is suspended from the rotunda ceiling, which is 142 feet above the floor.

The dome is divided into 12 vertical panels. At the base of the panels are paintings by Elmer Garnsey containing zodiac signs to suggest the constellation in the skies above.

The allegorical story, *The Civilization of the Northwest* by Edward Simmons, is told in four large murals above the third floor.

L'ETOILE
DV
N...

Rotunda Alcove Statues

John B. Sanborn

William J. Colvill

James Shields

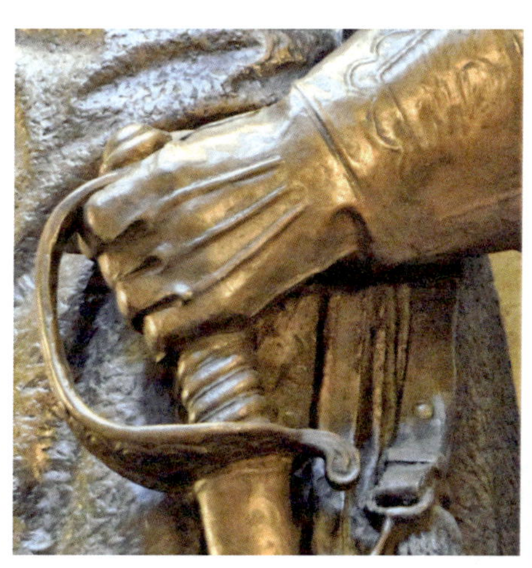

Alexander Wilkin

In the alcoves of the second-floor rotunda stand larger-than-life statues of Civil War heroes John B. Sanborn, Alexander Wilkin, William Colvill and James Shields, who were prominent figures in 19th-century Minnesota.

Minnesota sculptor John Karl Daniels created the statue of Alexander Wilkin and John B. Sanborn.

Chicago artist Frederick Cleveland Hibbard did the one of James Shields.

Minneapolis artist Catherine Backus sculpted William Colvill's image.

Grand Stairway

Located at the base of the skylight vaults above the grand staircases in the east and west wings are lunettes by Arthur Willett.

Each painting represents an important industry or activity that helped create the state's identity and success in the early 1900s.

They are *Logger* (pictured), *Horticulture, Huntress, Pioneer, Sowing, Dairy, Commerce, Winnowing, Stonecutting, Milling, Mining* and *Navigation*.

The *Logger* lunette in the east wing.

Grand Staircase Lunettes

Contemplative Spirits of the East is the lunette at the head of the east grand staircase.

Painted by Kenyon Cox, the intention is to symbolize the East as the land of contemplation and stability, contrasted with the progress and activity of the West.

The painting was installed in 1904.

The Sacred Flame is the lunette at the head of the west grand staircase.

Painted by Henry Oliver Walker, the theme is the passing of the flame from yesterday through today to tomorrow.

The central figure, called The Present, bows her head deep in emotion at the seriousness of her task.

The flame may be civilization, thought, or knowledge.

Walker's work was installed in 1904.

Contemplative Spirits of the East

Sacred Flame

Beautiful Marble

Twenty-seven different types of marble were used throughout the capitol. This creates a unique marbling pattern in the column.

Types of marble include Georgian; Tennessee; Skyros from Greece; Breche Violette, Old Convent Sienna, Levanto, and Moss, from Italy; Hauteville and Fleur de Peche, and French Echaillon from France; White Vermont and Verde Antique from Vermont; and Humidian from Africa.

House of Representatives Chamber

Above the Speaker of the House podium is a gold-painted, hand-carved plaster statuary, *Minnesota Spirit of Government*, created by Italian immigrants Carlos and Amerigo Brioschi.

The sculpture consists of a woman on a pedestal bearing the state seal. On the right are Sacagawea and a Native American chief, and to the left are early French explorers.

Below are the words "The Trail of the Pioneers Bore the Footprints of Liberty." The wall behind the sculpture bears the Latin phrase that reads, "The voice of the people is the voice of God."

The Chamber's glass ceiling is decorated with gold-leaf and stencils, including the letter M.

Senate Chamber

Minnesota: Granary to the World

In the Senate Chamber, there are two large 32-foot-wide murals painted by Edwin H. Blashfield.

Minnesota: Granary to the World shows Minnesota as a leader in agriculture.

Discoverers and Civilizers Led to the Source of the Mississippi depicts Native Americans and the spirit of Manitou at the headwaters of the Mississippi surrounded by discoverers and civilizers.

Four circular paintings by Elmer Garnsey and Arthur Willett depict *Courage, Equality, Justice* and *Freedom.*

Discoverers and Civilizers Led to the Source of the Mississippi

Supreme Court Chamber

The Supreme Court Chamber art above the judges' bench is *Moral and Divine Law* by John La Farge, depicting Moses on Mount Sinai representing human conscience and divine law. Other lunettes in the chamber are *The Relationship of Individual to the State*, *The Adjustment of the Conflicting Interests*, and *The Recording of the Precedents*.

L'ÉTOILE DU NORD

First Floor Hallway

Stencils on the walls and ceilings, reflecting a French artistic influence, display Minnesota symbols, including gophers, corn, wheat and Lady Slipper flowers.

At the end of the hallway, the state's motto, "L'Etoile du Nord," which means the Star of the North, is featured with a golden star and vases of Lady Slipper flowers.

Artists repainted the designs during the capitol restoration.

Third Floor Corridor Ceiling

Third floor corridor ceilings are decorated by paintings designed by Elmer Garnsey. They depict the four seasons.

Stencil design included ears of corn symbolic of the state's agriculture.

Garnsey created much of the artwork with quotations as appears on the next page.

Throughout the capitol, plaques and paintings present wisdom from former national leaders.

Minnesota National Leaders

Sculpture by Walker Hancock

Sculpture by George Bassett

Bronze busts of Warren Burger, left, and Hubert H. Humphrey, right, honor two Minnesota leaders who served their state and country. Burger was an attorney and jurist who served on the Supreme Court as the 15th Chief Justice of the United States from 1969-1986. He was an Assistant Attorney General prior to being appointed to the Supreme Court.

Humphrey was a politician who served as the 38th Vice President of the United States from 1965 to 1969 under the leadership of Lyndon B. Johnson. He served in the U.S. Senate twice, representing Minnesota from 1949 to 1964 and 1971 to 1978. He was the Senate Majority Whip for the last four years of his tenure.

Leaders of the People

Sculpture by George Bassett

Sculpture by JoAnne Bird

Rev. Martin Luther King Jr, left, and Chief Wabasha III, right, fought for the rights of their people.

King was one of the most prominent leaders in the civil rights movement from 1955 until his assassination in 1968. The American Baptist minister, activist and political philosopher participated in and led marches for the right to vote, desegregation, labor rights and other civil rights.

Wabasha was a prominent Dakota Sioux chief. In 1863, he opposed the Dakota War uprising from the start but struggled to gain support. After the tribe was relocated, he was known as head of the Santee Sioux. In the final years of his life, he helped his people rebuild their lives at the Santee Reservation in Nebraska.

Minnesota State Seal

The Great Seal of the State of Minnesota was originally adopted in 1858 following Minnesota's statehood. It has been modified several times by the state legislature, including 1971 and 1983. The legislature approved a redesign commission in 2023.

The seal's design symbolizes many important aspects of the state's history and culture, such as the growth of industry powered by Saint Anthony Falls, the state's Native American heritage, the importance of industries like lumber and agriculture, and the taming of the wilderness by the state's early pioneers.

The state motto, L'Etoile du Nord, meaning star of the north, is on the seal above the Native American and pioneer. The Mississippi River and St. Anthony Falls are depicted in the current seal to note the importance of these resources in transportation, industry and the settling of the state.

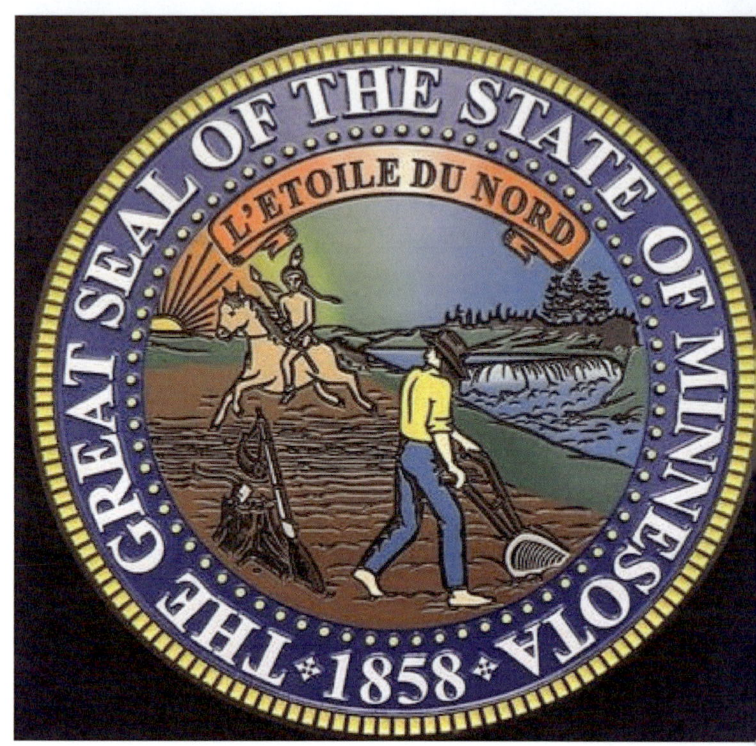

About the Photographer

Jane Moorman describes herself as an adventurer who loves to drive the backroads to see what there is to see.

During her 30-year journalism career, Jane honed her photographic skills as a photojournalist, including covering high school sporting events.

A friend once said, "I wish I could see the world as Jane sees it. Finding the beauty in things that most of us don't take time to see."

Upon retiring in 2021, Jane decided there was a lot of her native country she had not visited, including each state's capitol, so she began her journey of exploring the USA.

She currently lives in Albuquerque, New Mexico, but says her real home is on the road.